Speed-Reading At The Keyboard

Volume 3

By Edward Shanaphy, Stuart Isacoff
and Julie Jordan

©Copyright 1987 by Ekay Music, Inc.,
223 Katonah Avenue, Katonah, NY 10536.

Supplemental Volume
Reading Accompaniments

The ability to sight-read is a skill especially needed in accompanying situations. Keyboard players may be asked to play behind singers or instrumentalists at social gatherings, in church, at school . . . in any number of possible circumstances. Usually, the request is casual, but the response may be paralyzing anxiety.

This volume is designed to give you practice in reading typical accompaniment parts. Whether you actually spend time accompanying or not, they offer the opportunity to gain sight-reading expertise in a very common type of keyboard writing. The problems confronted in these pieces will appear in solo works as well.

This volume may be used in conjunction with the first two volumes of *Speed Reading At The Keyboard* material. Volume Three pieces are graded according to difficulty. As you progress through the first two volumes of the course, you should work your way through this supplementary volume until you reach a piece that is too difficult. At that point, resume your work through the program until you are ready for the next level of difficulty in the accompaniment book. By alternating between the course work and this collection, you will gain a wide range of practical experience and training to help you become a better sight-reader and a more knowledgeable musician.

Table of Contents

The Passion According To Saint Matthew

HEINRICH SCHUETZ

Lilliburlero

Henry Purcell

Ho! brod - er Teague, dost hear de de - cree? Lil - li - bur - le - ro
Dat we shall have a new dep - u - tie? Lil - li - bur - le - ro

bul - len a la. Le - ro, le - ro, lil - li - bur - le - ro,
bul - len a la.

Le - ro, le - ro, bul - len a la, Le - ro, le - ro,

lil - li - bur - le - ro, Le - ro, le - ro bul - len a la.

Le Tambourin

Jean Philippe Rameau

Allegro molto

Cradle Song

JOHANNES BRAHMS

Beautiful Isle of Somewhere

JOHN S. FEARIS

13

La Paloma

Sebastian Yradier

Andante

Slavonic Dance

Allegretto grazioso

ANTONIN DVORAK

Fine

D. C. al Fine

17

Divertimento No. 2

Wolfgang Amadeus Mozart

Tempo di menuetto

Menuetto D.C.

Vilia

FRANZ LEHAR

Duo No. 2

Ludwig van Beethoven

Deh Vieni, Non Tardar (Recitative)

Wolfgang Amadeus Mozart

bar - non ve - ni - te, il mio di - let - to!
wor - ry or fear shall mar our rap-ture!

a tempo

con anima

Oh co - me par, che all'a - mo - ro - so fo - co l'a - me - ni - tà del
Close to the heart of Na-ture's friend-ly pow-ers, del - i - cate, fra - grant

lo - co, la ter - ra e il ciel ri - spon - da!
flow - ers, the pine trees, the sky sur - round us.

p

con calore

Co - me la not - te i frut - ti miei se - con - da!
Aid - ing the lov - ers, night casts her veil a - round us!

Song Of India

NICHOLAS RIMSKY-KORSAKOV

Andantino

27

Andante Cantabile (Quartet, Op. 11)

Peter Ilyich Tchaikovsky

28

Finlandia

Jean Sibelius

Andante sostenuto

Melodie

JULES MASSENET

Lento ma non troppo

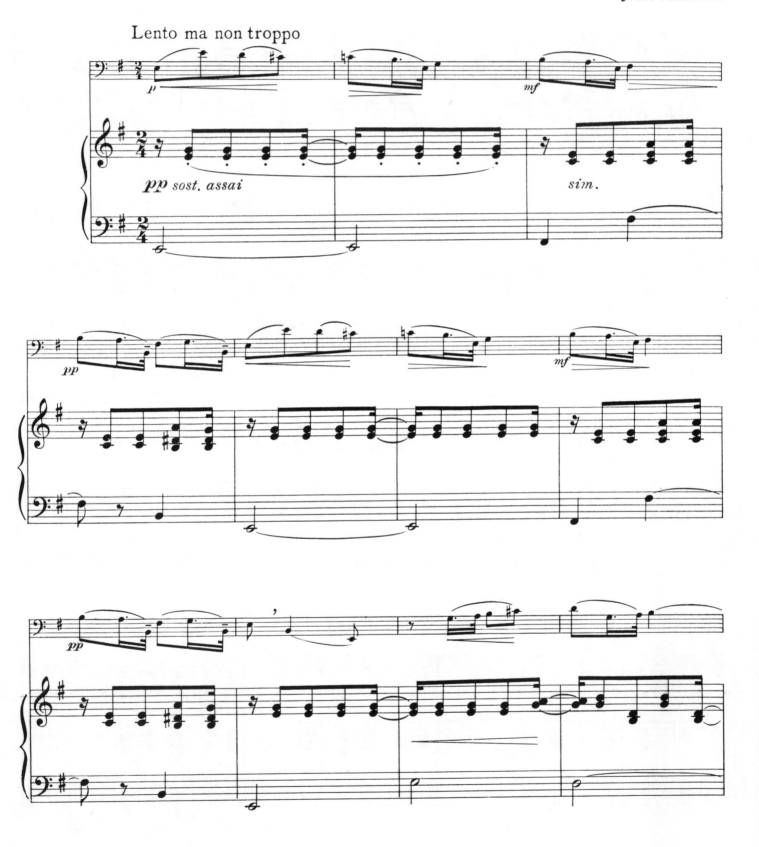

O Sole Mio!

Eduardo Di Capua

Aura Lee

George R. Poulton

La Cucaracha

TRADITIONAL

Fear No Danger To Ensue

from *Dido And Aeneas*

And the cares of life be - guil - ing. Fear no dan - ger to en -

sue, The He - ro loves as well as you. Cu - pids strew your

paths with flowers, Gath - er'd from E - ly - sian bowers. Fear no

dan - ger to en - sue, The He - ro loves as well as you.

La Golondina

TRADITIONAL

39

Bill Bailey

Brightly

HUGHIE CANNON

"Won't you come home, Bill Bail - ey? Won't you come home?"

She moans the whole day long. _____ "I'll do the

cook - ing, dar - ling, I'll pay the rent I know I've done you

wrong. _____ 'Mem - ber that rain - y eve that I drove you

out with noth - ing but a fine tooth comb? _____ I

know I'm to blame. Well ain't that a shame? Bill

Bail - ey won't you please come home?" _____

Take Me Out To The Ball Game

JACK NORWORTH, ALBERT VON TILZER

Crack - er Jack; I don't care if I nev - er get

back. Let me root, root, root for the home team. If

they don't win it's a shame. _____ For it's one, two,

cresc.

three strikes you're out at the old ball game. _____

f

Meet Me In St. Louis, Louis

Waltz Time

Andrew Sterling, Kerry Mills

Meet me in St. Lou - is, Lou - is,

Meet me at the fair. _____ Don't tell

me the lights are shin - ing an - y place but

there._____ We will dance the "hooch - ee kooch - ie,"_____

_____ I will be your toot - sie woot - sie._____

Meet me in St. Lou - is, Lou - is,

meet me at the fair._____

Green Grow The Rashes

Allegretto

JOSEF HAYDN

1. There's nought but care on ev – 'ry han', In ev – 'ry hour that pass – es, O; What
2. The warl' – ly race may rich – es chase, An' rich – es still may fly them, O; An'

sig – ni – fies the life o' man, An 'twere na for the lass – es, O?
tho' at last they catch them fast, Their hearts can ne'er en – joy them, O.

Green grow the rash – es, O! Green grow the rash – es, O! The

sweet - est hours that e'er I spend, Are spent a - mang the lass - es, O!

Green grow the rash - es, O! Green grow the rash - es, O! The

sweet - est hours that e'er I spend, Are spent a - mang the lass - es, O!

D. S.

The Pulse Of An Irishman

LUDWIG VAN BEETHOVEN

Vivace scherzando

place him where bul - lets fly thick - er and thick - er, You'll
brave be the sons, and still fair be the daugh - ters Thy

find him all cow - ard - ice scorn - - - ing.
meads and thy moun - tains a - dorn - - - ing!

And tho' a ball ____ should maim ____ poor Dar - by,
And tho' the east - ern sun ____ seems tar - dy,

Light at the heart he ral - lies on: "For - tune is cru - el, But
Tho' the pure light of know - ledge slow, Night and de - lu - sion And

No - rah, my jew - el, Is kind, and with smil - ing, All
dark - ling con - fu - sion, Like mists from the riv - er, Shall

sor - row be - guil - ing, Shall bid from our cab - in all
van - ish for - ev - er, And true I - rish hearts with warm

care to be gone; And how they will jig it, And
loy - al - ty glow; And proud ex - ul - ta - tion Burst

tug at the spi - got, On Pat - rick's day in the morn - ing."
forth from the na - tion On Pat - rick's day in the morn - ing.

For He's A Jolly Good Fellow

Lively

TRADITIONAL

1. For_____ he's a jol - ly good fel - low, For
2. We_____ won't go home un - til morn - ing, For

he's a jol - ly good fel - low, For he's a jol - ly good
won't go home un - til morn - ing, We won't go home un - til

fel - low, Which no - bod - y can de - ny!_____ Which
morn - ing, Till day - light doth ap - pear_____ Till

no - bod - y can de - ny,_____ Which no - bod - y can de -
day - light doth ap - pear,_____ Till day - light doth ap -

ny._____ For he's a jol - ly good fel - low, For
pear._____ We won't go home un - til morn - ing, We

he's a jol - ly good fel - low, For he's a jol - ly good
won't go home un - til morn - ing, We won't go home un - til

fel - low, Which no - bod - y can de - ny!_____
morn - ing, Till day - light doth ap - pear!_____

Morning Greeting

Franz Schubert

Moderato

1. Good morn - ing, love - ly mil - ler's maid, Why hide thy head as __
2. I on - ly crave a - far to __ gaze Up - on thy win - dow's __
1. Gu - ten Mor - gen, schö - ne Mül - le - rin! wo steckst du gleich das __
2. O lass mich nur von fer - ne __ steh'n, nach dei - nem lie - ben __

if a - fraid, That charm - ing face __ con - ceal - ing?
shin - ing rays, Tho' dis - tant, 'tis __ my pleas - ure.
Köpf - chen hin, als wär' dir was ge - sche - hen?
Fen - ster seh'n, von fer - ne, ganz __ von fer - ne!

Say, doth my greet - ing vex thee so, And __
I fain at thy small door would see That __
Ver - driesst dich denn mein Gruss so schwer? ver -
Du blon - des Köpf - chen, komm her - vor! her -

doth my look per - plex thee so? Then hence must I __ be
fair young head so dear to me, And morn - ing stars of
stört dich denn mein Blick so sehr? So muss ich wie - der
vor aus eu - rem run - den Thor, ihr blau - en Mor - gen-

steal - ing, Then hence must I __ be steal - ing, must I __ be
a - zure, And morn - ing stars of a - zure, the stars of
ge - hen, so muss ich wie - der ge - hen, wie - der
ster - ne, ihr blau - en Mor - gen-ster - ne, ihr Mor - gen-

steal - ing.
a - zure.
ge - hen.
ster - ne.

Mighty Lak' A Rose

ETHELBERT NEVIN

57

'Tis The Last Rose Of Summer

FELIX MENDELSSOHN

'Tis the last rose of __ sum - mer, Left __ bloom - ing __ a - lone; All her love - ly __ com - pan - ions Are __ fad - ed __ and __ gone; No __ flow'r of her kin - dred, No __ rose - bud is

nigh To re - flect back her blush-es, Or give sigh for sigh.

1. 'Tis the last rose of summer,
   Left blooming alone;
   All her lovely companions
   Are faded and gone;
   No flow'r of her kindred,
   No rosebud is nigh
   To reflect back her blushes,
   Or give sigh for sigh.

2. I'll not leave thee, thou lone one,
   To pine on the stem;
   Since the lovely are sleeping,
   Go sleep thou with them;
   Thus kindly I scatter
   Thy leaves o'er the bed,
   Where thy mates of the garden
   Lie scentless and dead.

3. So soon may I follow,
   When friendships decay,
   And from love's shining circle
   The gems drop away!
   When true hearts lie wither'd
   And fond ones are flown,
   Oh! who would inhabit
   This bleak world alone?

Symphony No. 3 (Second Movement)

JOHANNES BRAHMS

Sonata Movement

WILLEM DE FESCH

Larghetto
Aria

Hello! My Baby

With a Bounce

JOSEPH HOWARD, IDA EMERSON

Hel - lo, my ba - by, hel - lo my hon - ey,

Hel - lo, my rag - time gal! Send me a kiss by

wire; Ba - by my heart's on fire!

If you re - fuse me, hon - ey, you'll lose me, Then you'll be left a -

lone; Oh, ba - by, tel - e - phone and tell me I'm your

1. own. Hel-lo! Hel - lo! Hel-lo there! 2. own.

After The Ball

CHARLES K. HARRIS

Moderately

After The Ball is o - ver,

After the break of morn,_____

After the danc - ers' leav - ing,

After the stars are gone;_____

Man - y a heart is ach - ing,

If you could read them all; Man - y the

hopes that have van - ished, Af - ter The

1.
Ball.

2.
Ball.

The Red Haired Girl

TRADITIONAL

Ma - ny girls I know, with long tres - ses that flow, And ma - ny are the maids, with their hair all a-curl— But like fields of wav-ing corn are her tres - ses in the morn And the rud - dy gold-en glint of the red-haired girl.

Praise no Span-ish maids, or French with their braids, It's an
Ir - ish col-leen sure makes my heart in a whirl, And I think the fair - est sight, that has
brought me most de-light, Is the sheen up - on the locks of my red-haired girl.

69

Barb'ra Allen

Allegretto

TRADITIONAL

1. 'Twas in and a - bout the ___ Mar - t'mas ___ time, When the

green leaves were ___ a - fall - ing, That Sir John Graeme in the

West ___ coun - try, Fell in love with Bar - b'ra ___ Al - lan. He

sent his man down thro' the town, To the place where she was

dwell - ing — "O haste, and come to my

mas - ter dear, — Gin — ye be Bar - b'ra Al - lan."

D. S. (or segue)

Waltz

Tempo di Waltz

CHARLES GOUNOD

cantabile
mf

mf

Symphony No. 5 (First Movement)

Peter Ilyich Tchaikovsky

77

A Picture Of Her Face

SCOTT JOPLIN

This life is ver - - y sad to me, a sor - row fills my

I'll ne'er for - get the days I've pass'd, with Grace, so kind and

heart,_____ My sto - ry I will tell to you, from me my

true,_____ She was to me each day more joy than all the

love did part,_____ The vil - lage church bell sad - ly tolled, the
girls I knew,_____ My love for her will ne'er grow cold though

one I loved had died,_____ She was a treas - ure more than
she has passed a - way,_____ I'll love her still when I am

gold, when she was by my side._____ But now she's gone be -
old e'en to my dy - ing day._____ But now I must con -

- yond re - call, in a si - lent tomb she sleeps,_____ The
- tent my - self, her mem - o - ry to love,_____ For

one I loved yet best of all has left me here to weep;____ Though
Grace the dar-ling of my heart is in the land a-bove;____ But

death so ruth-less stole my love, my dear and on-ly Grace,____ I've
still to cheer me at my home an im-age of dear Grace,____ Is

yet a treas-ure in this world, A pic-ture of her face.____ It
all the treas-ure I now have, A pic-ture of her face.____

brings joy to me ____ when oft-times sad at heart,____ Her

pic - ture I can see,＿＿＿ And sad thoughts then de - part;＿＿＿ Al -

- though my love is dead,＿＿＿ My on - ly dar - ling Grace,＿＿＿ My

eyes are oft - times looking on A picture of her face.＿＿＿

81

Serenade

Victor Herbert

82

You're The Flower Of My Heart, Sweet Adeline

RICHARD GERARD / HARRY ARMSTRONG

Andante

In the eve - ning when I sit a - lone a - dream - ing _____ Of days gone
I can see your smil - ing face as when we wan - dered _____ Down by the

by, love _____ to me so dear. There's a
brook - side _____ just you and I, And it

pic - ture that in fan - cy oft ap - pear - ing, _____ Brings back the
seems so real at times 'till I a - wak - en _____ To find all

time love_____ when you were near.   It is then I won-der where you are   my
van - ished_____ a dream gone by;   If we meet some-time in af - ter years   my

dar - ling,   And   if   your   heart   to   me   is   still   the
dar - ling,   I   trust   that   I   will   find   your   love   still

same,   For   the   sigh - ing   wind   and   night - in - gale   a -
mine.   Tho'   my   heart   is   sad   and   clouds   a - bove   are

sing - ing_____   Are   breath - ing   on   ly_____   your   own   sweet   name._____
hov - 'ring_____   The   sun   a - gain   love_____   for   me   would   shine._____

CHORUS

Sweet A - del - ine, _____ My A - del - ine _____ At night, Dear-

heart _____ For you I pine, _____ In all my

dreams, _____ Your fair face beams, You're the

flow - er of my heart, Sweet A - del - ine.

Funiculi Funicula

LUIGI DENZA

86

Sweet Adeline

RICHARD GERARD, HARRY ARMSTRONG

Slowly

Sweet A - del - ine, My A - del - ine, At night, dear

heart, For you I pine; In all my dreams your fair face

beams, You're the flow - er of my heart. Sweet A - del - ine.

Harrigan

GEORGE M. COHAN

Who is the man who will spend or will e - ven lend?
Who is the man nev - er stood for a gad a - bout?

Har - ri - gan, That's me! ___ Who is your friend when you
Har - ri - gan, That's me! ___ Who is the man that the

find that you need a friend? Har - ri - gan, That's me! ___ For
town's sim - ply mad a - bout? Har - ri - gan, That's me! ___ The

I'm just as proud of my name you see, As an Em-per-or, Czar or a
la-dies and ba-bies are fond of me, I'm fond of them, too, in re-

King, could be: Who is the man helps a
turn, you see: Who is the gent that's de-

man ev-'ry time he can? Har-ri-gan, That's me!___
ser-ving a mon-u-ment? Har-ri-gan, That's me!___

CHORUS

H - A dou-ble R - I - G-A-N spells Har-ri-gan,

Proud of all the I-rish blood that's in me; Div-il a man can say a word a-

gin me. H - A dou-ble R - I -

G - A - N, you see,_____ Is a name that a shame nev-er

has been con-nect-ed with Har-ri-gan, That's me!__ me!__

91

Air

Johann Sebastian Bach

The Cavalier

from *The Merry Widow*

FRANZ LEHAR

SON.

Look up, maid_en, mark him well! Leave the dan_cers lone_ly,

SON.

He may like you, who can tell, If he sees you on_ly!

DANILO.

So she glan_ces shy and sly, And she meets the horse_man's eye!

SONIA.

Not a word she says, but still, He can take her if he will!

96

I Love You So
from *The Merry Widow*

FRANZ LEHAR

DAN. true, You love me so! And to the mu-sic's

SONIA
rit:

Valse lento

SON. chime, My heart is beat-ing time, As if to give a

SON. sign, That it would say, Be mine, be mine! Though our

pp

SON. lips may say no word. Yet in the heart a voice is heard. You can-not choose but

SON.

know   I   love   you   so.____

p animato

Ped.   *

Ped.   *   simile

SONIA

allargando

Ev - 'ry   touch   of   fin - gers

DANILO.

Ev - 'ry   touch   of   fin - gers

allargando

Ped.   *

100

Concert Piece No. 2

Felix Mendelssohn

Silver Threads Among The Gold

HART P. DANKS

The Fishermaiden

FRANZ SCHUBERT

Poco Allegro

Thou love-ly Fish-er-maid - en, Steer now thy boat to
Du schö-nes Fischer - mäd - chen, trei - be den Kahn an's

land, ___ Come to me and sit ___ be - side me, We'll
Land; ___ komm zu mir und se-tze dich nie - der, wir

whis-per hand in hand, Come to me and sit ___ be - side me, We'll
ko - sen, Hand in Hand, komm zu mir und se - tze dich nie - der, wir

whis - per hand in hand,___ We'll whis - per hand in hand.
ko - sen, Hand in Hand,___ wir ko - sen, Hand in Hand.

Then
Leg'

lay thy head on my bo - som, Fear naught, but trust thou in me,___
an mein Herz___ dein Köpf - chen und fürch - te dich nicht zu sehr;___

dim.

For thou dost trust___ all fear - less,
ver - trau'st du dich___ doch sorg - los

Dai - ly the storm-y sea, For thou dost trust all fear - less,
täg - lich dem wil - den Meer, ver-trau'st du dich doch sorg - los

Dai - ly the storm-y sea, _____ Dai - ly the storm-y sea.
täg - lich dem wil - den Meer, _____ täg - lich dem wil - den Meer!

My
Mein

dim.

heart is like the sea there, Hath storm, and ebb, and flow, _____
Herz gleicht ganz dem Mee - re, hat Sturm und Ebb' und Fluth, _____

And many a pearl may be there, With—in— the depths be-
und man-che schö-ne Per-le in sei-ner Tie-fe

low,　　And many a pearl may be there, With-in— the depths be-
ruht,　　und man-che schö-ne Per-le in sei-ner Tie-fe

low,— With-in— the depths be-low.—
ruht,— in sei-ner Tie-fe ruht.—

dim.

111

Thy Hand, Belinda
from *Dido And Aeneas*

HENRY PURCELL

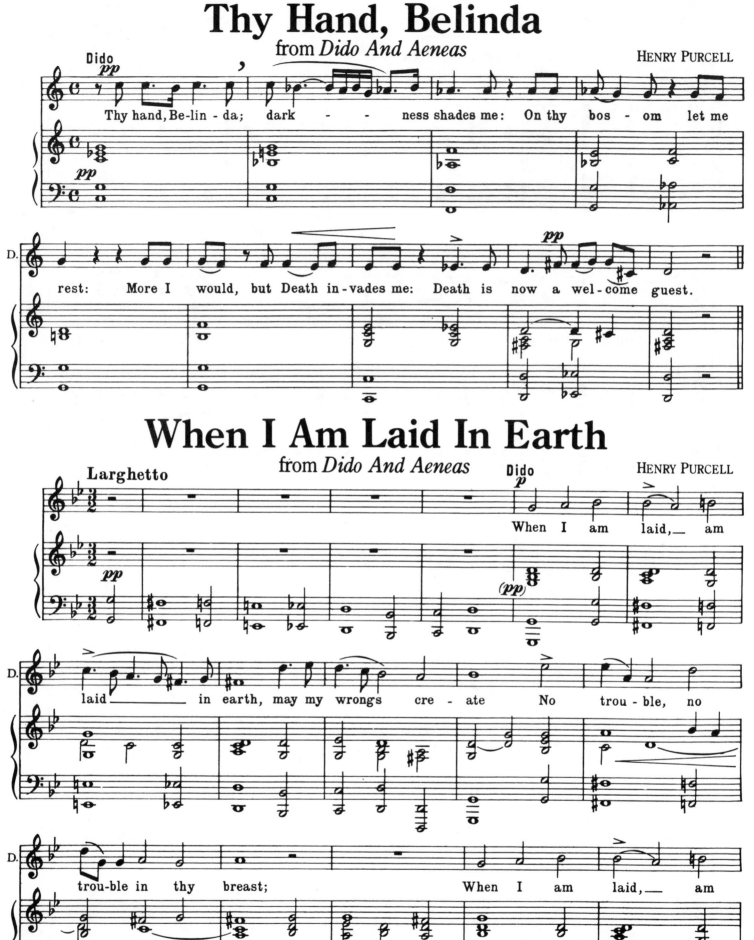

Thy hand, Be-lin-da; dark - - ness shades me: On thy bos-om let me rest: More I would, but Death in-vades me: Death is now a wel-come guest.

When I Am Laid In Earth
from *Dido And Aeneas*

HENRY PURCELL

When I am laid,— am laid— in earth, may my wrongs cre-ate No trou-ble, no trou-ble in thy breast; When I am laid,— am

laid _____ in earth, may my wrongs cre - ate No trou - ble, no

trou - ble in thy breast; Re - mem - ber me, re - mem - ber me,

but ah!__ for - get ___ my fate, Re - mem - ber me, but ah!_____

for - get my__ fate.

Si Le Bonheur A Sourire

from *Faust*

CHARLES GOUNOD

Si   le bon-heur   à   sou-ri - re   t'in-
When to   thy vis-ion life   ap-pears sweet - ly

vi - te, Joy-eux a - lors, je sens un doux   é - moi,   Si la dou-
smil-ing, Then all a - bout me seems to smile   on me,   But if sad

leur__ tac - ca - ble, Mar-gue - ri - te, Ô Mar - gue - ri - te, ô Mar-gue-
tears come and naught seems life be - guil-ing, Then, O my lov'd one, then, O my

ri - te, je pleure a - lors, je pleu - re com - me toi.
lov'd one, Then I will weep for thee, will weep for thee.

Com - me deux
As two fond

p

cresc. *cresc.* *dim.* *p*

fleurs sur u - ne mê - me ti - ge, No - tre des - tin suivait le mê - me
flow'r-ets on one stem u - nit - ed, So link'd by des-ti - ny our hearts are

cours, De tes cha-grins en frè - re je m'af-fli - ge, Ô Mar-gue-
bound, Should ev - er sor-rows come or hopes be blight - ed, Then ev - er

ri - te, ô Mar - gue-ri - te, Com-me u - ne sœur je t'ai-me-rai tou-
faith-ful, then ev - er faith - ful, then I shall faith-ful, ev-er true be

jours, je ___ t'ai - me - rai tou - jours, je ___
found, ev - er faith - ful, ev - er true be found, ev - er

t'ai - me - rai tou - jours!
faith-ful, ev - er true be found!

116

Old French Dance

118

Ave Maria

GIUSEPPE VERDI

Pre - ga per chi a - do - ran - do a te si pro - stra,
Pray thou for them who kneel - ing do a - dore___ thee,

Pre - ga___ pel pec - ca - tor, per l'in no - cen - te,
Pray thou___ for sin - ners, too, pray for the ho - ly,

E pel de - bo - le op - pres - so e pel pos - sen - te, Mi - se - ro an -
Pray for great and might - y, pray for meek and low - ly, Pray for the

ch'es - so, tua pie - tà di - mo - stra.
mourn - ers ly - ing prone be - fore___ thee.

Pre - ga per chi sot - to l'ol - trag - gio pie - ga la fron - te e
Pray— for all who bow 'neath the yoke of cru - el op - pres - sion,

sot - to la mal-va - gia sor - te; Per noi, per noi, tu
for the poor and bro - ken - heart - ed, Pray thou for us, O

pre - ga, pre - ga__ sem - pre e nel l'o - ra d'el - la__
Ma - ry, pray for us al - ways! And in that hour__ when we in

mor - te no - stra, Pre - ga per noi, pre - ga per noi, per
death are ly - ing, Pray for our souls, pray for our souls, our

Amour, Que Veux-Tu De Moi?

from *Amadis*

Andante espressivo

GIOVANNI BATTISTE LULLY

A_mour, que veux-tu de moi? Mon cœur n'est pas fait pour toi, Mon
O love, what wilt thou with me? My heart is not made for thee, My

cœur n'est pas fait pour toi! Non, ne t'oppo-se pas au pen-chant qui m'entraîne, Je
heart is not made for thee! No, do not thou oppose the de-sires that possess me, For

suis ac-cou-tu-mée à res-sen-tir la hai-ne, Je
I am wont to feel the pang of hate op-press me. A

ne veux ins-pi-rer que l'hor-reur et l'ef-froi. A - mour, que veux-tu de
source a-lone of ter-ror and dread I shall be. O Love, what wilt thou with

moi? Mon cœur au - rait trop de pei - ne À suivre u - ne dou - ce
me? My heart would be too much troub-led, So will - ing a slave to

loi, C'est mon sort d'être in - hu - mai - ne; A - mour, que veux-tu de
be; 'Tis my fate to be hard-heart-ed; O Love, what wilt thou with

moi? Mon cœur n'est pas fait pour toi, Mon cœur n'est pas fait pour toi!
me? My heart is not made for thee, My heart is not made for thee!

125

The Foggy Dew

TRADITIONAL

In moderate time

1. A - down the hill I went one morn, A love-ly maid I spied, Her hair was bright as the dew that wets Sweet An - ner's ver - dant side, And where go ye, sweet maid? said I, She raised her eyes of blue, And smiled and said "The boy I wed I'm to meet in the fog-gy dew."

2. Go hide your blooms ye ro-ses red And droop ye li-lies rare, Or
3. A-down the hill I went at morn, A-sing-ing I did go, A-

you must pale for ve-ry shame, Be-fore a maid so fair. Said
down the hill I went at morn She an-swer'd soft and low "Yes,

I "Dear maid, will you be my bride?" Be-neath her eyes of blue, She
I will be your own dear bride And I know that you'll be true" Then

smiled and said, "The boy I wed I'm to meet in the fog-gy dew."
sighed in my arms, and all her charms Were hid in the fog-gy dew.

Nur Fur Natur
from *Der Lustige Krieg*

Gemäßigtes Walzertempo

JOHANN STRAUSS

Nur____ für Na - tur____ heg-te sie____ Sym-pa - thie,____ un-ter Bäu - men_ sü - ßes

Träu - men_ lieb-te Grä - fin Me - la - nie.____ Ach,____ wel-che Lust____ füllt das Herz,

____ hebt die Brust,____ wenn im Schat - ten_ grü-ner Mat - ten_ man so hin-schwärmt un - be-

wußt.____ Ihr Cou - sin war sehr jung und ga - lant,____ man be - haup - tet so-gar in-tres-

128

sant,_____ selbst der Graf fand ihn äu - ßerst scharmant,_____ lud ihn zu sich sehr oft aufs Land.

Man zog häu - fig hin-aus ins Re - vier,_____ denn die Jagd macht der Grä - fin Plä-sier;

_ welch ro-man - tisch Ge-fühl, welch ein Bild,_____ zeigt im Wald sich ed - les Wild. Ja,

nur_____ für Na-tur_____ hegte sie_____ Sympa - thie,_____ un-ter Bäu - men_ sü - ßes Träu - men

_ lieb - te Grä - fin Me - la - nie._____

Piff, paff, puff! Rasch den Hahn ge - spannt, _____ sol - che Jagd ist

doch a - mü - sant. _____ Der Herr Graf sieht _____ dort in der Au _____

jetzt ei - nen Hirsch und ver - gißt sei - ne Frau. Eilt ihm nach ü - ber Stock und _

Stein, _____ der Cou - sin bleibt mit ihr al - lein. _____ Dort ein Schuß, bum,

und hier ein Kuß, _____ doch nun ga - lant ich schwei - gen muß. _____

Nur___ für Na - tur___ heg-te sie___ Sym-pa - thie,___ un-ter Bäu - men ___ sü - ßes Träu - men___ lieb-te Grä - fin Me - la - nie.___ Nun___ liegt ge- fällt___ dort der Hirsch;___ Graf als Held___ bricht durch Ran - ken,___ kommt zu dan - ken ___ dem Cou-sin, daß er Grä-fin so a - müsiert.

When You Were Sweet Sixteen

JAMES THORNTON

Slowly *(with expression)*

When first I saw the love-light in your eye ____ I
Last night I dreamt I held your hand in mine ____ And

dreamt the world held naught but joy for me ____ And e-ven though we drift-ed far a-
once a-gain you were my hap-py bride ____ I kissed you as I did In Auld Lang

part ____ I nev-er dream but what I dream of thee: ____
Syne ____ As to the church we wan-dered side by side: ____

Ballad style
CHORUS

I love you as I ne-ver loved be-fore ____ Since first I met you on the vil-lage

132

green   Come to me or my dream of love is o'er _____   I

love you as I loved you When you were sweet, when you were sweet six - teen.

rit

Fox-trot version
CHORUS

I love you as I ne-ver loved be - fore _____   Since first I met you on the vil-lage green _____

mf

Come to me or my dream of love is o'er _____   I love you as I loved you _____

| 1 | 2 |

_When you were sweet, _____ when you were sweet six-teen.   I teen. _____

rit

133

Gern Hab' Ich Die Frau'n Gekusst

from *Paganini*

FRANZ LEHAR

Ich lie - be heiß, _____ doch treu bin ich nicht sehr, _____ bin ein Mann, _____ nicht viel dran. Liebchen fein: _____ ich schau auch and-re an! _____ Ich kenn' der wahr-haf - ten Lie - be Glut, _____ ich weiß wie weh oft die Falsch-heit tut, _____ ich kenn' die Won-nen, be - gon - nen mit Freud, _____ ich sah ihr Wen-den und En-den mit Leid! Ich kenn' die Lie - be in Dur und Moll, _____ ich kenn' sie

se - lig, ver - rückt und toll, ___ ich schau' er - wa-chend und la - chend zu - rück ___

meno

Allegretto moderato (♩=52)

rit.

___ und such im Rau-sche, im Tau-sche mein Glück!

prit.

sehr weich
p a tempo

ppp

Gern ___ hab' ich die Frau'n ge - küßt, ___ hab' nie ge -

ppp a tempo

fragt, ___ ob es ge - stat - tet ist, ___ dach - te mir: ___ nimm sie

dir, ___ küß' sie nur, ___ da - zu sind sie ja hier! ___

meno

meno

p

mf

Ach, Ich Hab' Sie Ja Nur

from *Der Bettelstudent*

CARL MILLOECKER

Allegro vivace

1. Und da soll man noch ga - lant sein ge - gen schö - ne - res Ge - schlecht, kat - zen -
2. Die - se a - dels - stol - ze Da - me war be - lei - digt durch den Kuß, wäh - rend

buk-keln und schar-mant sein, spie-len den er-geb-nen Knecht! Ei - nen Hel - den, den in
das doch nur Re - kla - me ih - ren Rei-zen ma-chen muß! Wenn man sonst mich in - sul -

Po - len wie in Sach-sen je - der kennt, den Wol - hy-nien und Po - do-lien nur mit
tier-te, rächt' ich's im - mer blu-tig schnell; Arm und Bei - ne am-pu - tier-te ich wohl

höch-ster Ach-tung nennt; der am Pruth und an der Weich-sel, an der El - be Sieg er-
zwan-zig im Du - ell; ha, ich wü - te, schäu-me, ra - se, dür - ste nach Sa - tis-fak-

rang, der bei Grod - no, Baut-zen, Wur-zen al - le Fein - de nie-der-
tion, und ich schwör's bei die - ser Na - se, sie be - kommt noch ih - ren

Mäßiges Walzertempo

zwang! Ha! _____ Die-sen Hel - den, _____ nie ge - schla - gen, _____
Lohn! Ha! _____ Die Bla - ma - ge _____ zu ver - schmer - zen _____

_____ ü - ber - all _____ hoch ver - ehrt, _____ durft ein Weib zu _____ schla - gen
_____ ich zu lä - - cheln mich zwang, _____ doch es tob - te _____ Wut im

wa - gen; _____ der Ge - dan - ke _____ mich em - pört! _____ Die Er -
Her - zen _____ und das Lä - cheln _____ es miß - lang! _____ Jam - mer -

in - ner - ung macht mich be - ben, mich so tät - lich zu in - sul - tie - ren, doch
vol - le Gri - mas - sen schnitt ich, nicht zu zei - gen, wie mir zu Mut, nahm es

soll sie et - was von mir er - le - ben, mei - ne Ra - che spü - ren! War es denn
spaß - haft zwar, doch im In - nern litt ich, mir war gar - nicht gut! Und's war, wenn den

ei - gent - lich gar so fürch - ter - lich, war - um ich so schwer ge - büßt: Ha! _____
Grund man hört, nicht der Re - de wert, was ihr wi - der - fah - ren ist. Ha! _____

_____ Ach ich hab _____ sie ja nur _____ auf die Schul - - ter ge -
_____ Ach ich hab _____ sie doch nur _____ auf die Schul - - ter ge -

küßt, _____ ach ich hab _____ sie ja nur _____ auf die Schul - - ter ge -
küßt, _____ ach ich hab _____ sie doch nur _____ auf die Schul - - ter ge -

Allegro

küßt! Hier hab ich den Schlag ver-spürt mit dem Fä-cher ins Ge-sicht!
küßt! Schau-der-haft bin ich bla-miert, al - le Welt heut da-von spricht!

Allegretto

1.-2. Mir ist man-ches schon pas - siert, a - ber so et-was noch nicht, a - ber

so et-was noch nicht! Mir ist man-ches schon pas - siert, a - ber so et-was, so et-was,

so 'was nicht!

(poco più mosso)

Thank You, My Friends

W.A. MOZART

Nehmt mei-nen Dank, ihr hol - den
Thank you, my friends, I sing it

Gön - ner! So feu - rig, als mein Herz ihn spricht, euch laut zu sa - gen, kön - nen
proud - ly, As ar - dent thanks as heart can speak; A man may sing your prais - es

Män - ner, ich, nur ein Weib, ich, nur ein Weib, ver-mag es nicht. Doch
loud - ly, But wom-an's voice, my wom-an's voice is du - ly meek. Be-

glaubt, doch glaubt, ich werd' in mei - nem Le-ben, glaubt, ichwerd' in mei - nem
lieve my mem - o-ry will keep you ev - er, Mem - o - ry will keep you

Le - ben nie-mals ver-ges-sen eu - re Huld;
ev - er Cher-ished, for kind-ness shown___ a friend:

blieb' ich,   blieb' ich, so wä - re mein Be - stre - ben, — sie zu ver -
Stay - ing,   I would have made it my en - deav - or — To serve you

die - nen,   doch   Ge - duld;   blieb' ich,
glad - ly   till   the end,   Stay - ing,

blieb' ich, so wä - re mein Be - stre - ben, — sie zu ver - die - nen,
I would have made it my en - deav - or — To serve you glad - ly,

doch Ge - duld, Ge - duld, Ge -
yes, to serve un - til the

duld!
end.

Von An - be -
Since time be -

ginn war ste - tes Wan - dern der Mu - sen und der Künst - ler
gan, the Fates de - cid - ed That art - ists con - stant - ly must

Los; mir geht es so wie al - len An - dern, fort aus des
roam, And so with me, by Mus - es guid - ed, I leave my

Va - ter - lan - des Schoss sch' ich mich von dem Schick - - sal
fa - ther - land and home. My des - ti - ny has thus _____ de -

lei - - - ten. Doch glaubt, doch
creed _____ it, But oh! in

glaubt es mir, in je - dem Reich, doch glaubt es mir, in je - dem
ev - 'ry land that calls and lures, In ev - 'ry land that calls and

Reich, wo - hin ich geh', zu al - len Zei - ten
lures, Wher - e'er I go, I shall __ con - cede __ it,

bleibt im-mer-dar, bleibt im-mer-dar mein Herz bei euch,_ mein
You hold me yet, You hold me, for my heart is yours,_ My

Herz bei euch, bleibt im-mer-dar, bleibt im-mer-dar mein Herz bei
heart is_ yours, You hold me yet, You hold me, for my heart is

euch,_ bleibt im-mer - dar_ mein Herz bei_ euch, bei_
yours, You hold me yet,_ My_ heart is_ yours, my_

euch, bei_ euch.
heart is_ yours.

147

Shepherd's Lament

Moderato

Franz Schubert

Full man - y a day_ I lin - ger On yon - der mountain's
Da dro - ben auf je - nem Ber - ge da steh' ich tau - send-

brow, Up-on_ my crook all id - ly lean - ing, And gaze in the val-ley be-
mal, an mei - nem Sta - be hin-ge-bo - gen, und schau-e hin-ab in das

low.
Thal.

Then fol-low my flock as they're graz_ - ing, My
Dann folg'ich der wei-den-den Heer - de, mein

dog ev - er watches them well,
Hündchen be-wah-ret mir sie,

And find_ my-self in the val - ley,
ich bin_ her - un - ter ge - kom - men

Yet how, I nev-er can tell,   The

und weiss doch sel - ber nicht wie,   Da

cresc.   *p*   *pp*

mead - ow lies spread be - fore   me,   With   love - ly flow'rs of

ste - het von schö - nen Blu - - men,   da   steht   die gan - ze

ev - e - ry hue;   I   gath - er them, tho' without   know - ing Whom I shall

Wie - se so voll,   ich   bre - che sie, oh - ne zu   wis - sen wem ich sie

give _____ them to.   And rain,   and thun - der, and

ge - _____ ben soll.   Und Re - gen, Sturm und Ge -

f

light - ning I heed not un - der the tree,
wit - ter ver - pass' ich un - ter dem Baum.

But fondest hopes ev - er de - ceive me, Yon door is ne'er open'd to
Die Thü - re dort blei - bet ver - schlossen, doch al - les ist lei - der ein

me. Bright arch - ing a - bove_ yon cot - tage A
Traum. Es ste - het ein Re - gen - bo - gen wohl

rain - bow gay_ doth stand, But she has de - part - ed who dwelt there, And
ü - ber je - nem Haus, sie a - ber ist fort - ge - zo - gen und

far a-way o-ver the land.   Far o-ver the land,— or
weit in das Land hin-aus.   Hin-aus in das Land— und

e - ven, Per-haps, far o-ver the sea; Go fur-ther, my sheep, pass by,— pass
wei - ter, viel-leicht gar ü-ber die See; vor-ü-ber, ihr Scha-fe, nur— vor-

by— it; Poor shepherd, ah; woe— is me; Go fur-ther, my sheep, pass by;— pass
ü - ber, dem Schä-fer is gar— so weh, vor-ü-ber, ihr Scha-fe, nur— vor-

by— it; Poor shepherd, ah, woe— is me!
ü - ber, dem Schä-fer ist gar— so weh!

151

Silence! You've Conquered!
(Ah, Do Not Let Us Part!)

W.A. MOZART

Recitativo Didone / Andantino

Ba - sta, vin - ces - ti, ec - co - ti il fo - glio.
Si - lence! you've con - quered! Here it is, your let - ter.

Ve - di quan - to t'a - do - ro an - co - ra in - gra - to.
See how much, though you're thank - less, I still a - dore you.

Con
A

un tuo sguar - do so - lo mi to - glio - gni di - fe - sa e mi dis -
sin - gle look a - larms me And, leav - ing me de - fense - less, With ease dis -

ar - mi;
arms me.

ed ai cor di tra-dir-mi, ed ai
By your glance I am shak-en. Will your

cor di tra-dir - mi?
heart play the trai - tor?

e poi la - sciar - mi?
Am I for - sak - en?

Aria

Andantino espressivo

Ah non la-sciar-mi,
Ah! do not let us

no,___ bell' I-dol mi - o, bell' I-dol mi -
part,___ My own Be-lov - ed, my own Be-lov -

153

o; di chi — mi fi - de - rò, — se tu — m'in -
ed. To whom — will go my heart — If you — de -

gan - ni? Ah non la - sciar - mi,
ceive — me? Ah! Love, we must not

no, ah no, non la - sciar - mi; di chi — mi fi - de -
part; Ah! Love, nev - er leave me; To whom — will go my

rò, — se tu — m'in - gan - ni? di
heart — If you — de - ceive — me? To

chi ___ mi fi-de-rò, ___ di chi, ___ se
whom ___ will go my heart, ___ to whom, ___ If

tu m'in-gan - ni, se tu m'in-gan -
you de-ceive ___ me, If you de-ceive ___

ni?
me?

Di vi - ta man-che - re - i, di vi - ta man-che-
The dread of part-ing fills me, To say fare-well, Love,

re - i nel dir - ti: ad - di - o, nel dir - ti: ad - tle
chills me; And lost hope now kills me, While Death's man - tle

di - o,
stills me.

che vi - ver non po -
If long - ing_ could re -

tre - i, che vi - ver_ non po - tre - i fra - tle
cap - ture Our hap - pi - ness that van - ished, We_

tan - ti af - fan - ni, fra tan - ti af - fan - ni!
might find new rap - ture, And heart - ache be ban - ished.

Recitativo

Allegretto

Ah no, non la-sciar-mi! ah no, non la-sciar-mi!
Ah! Love, do not leave me, Ah! Love, do not leave me.

Andante espressivo

Ah non la-sciar-mi, no, ___ bell' I - dol mi - o, bell'
Ah! do not let us part, ___ My own Be - lov - ed, my

I - dol mi - o; di chi ___ mi fi - de - rò, ___ se
own Be - lov - ed. To whom ___ will go my heart, ___ If

tu ___ m'in - gan - ni?
you ___ de - ceive ___ me?

Ah
Ah!

157

non la-sciar-mi, no, ___ ah no, non la-sciar-mi, ah
Love, we must not part, ___ Ah! Love, nev-er leave me; Ah! ___

no, di chi mi fi - de - rò, ___ se tu, ___ se
Love, to whom will go my heart, ___ to whom, If

tu ___ m'in gan - - ni? di chi mi fi - de-
you ___ de - ceive ___ me? To whom will go my

rò, ___ di chi, ___ se tu, ___ se tu, ___ se tu m'in-
heart, to whom, If you, ___ if you, ___ a - las! would

158

gan - - ni? se tu m'in-gan - ni, se
leave _____ me? We must not thus __ part,

tu m'in-gan - - ni? Ah non la-
own Be - lov - - ed; To whom will

sciar - mi, no, ah non la-sciar - - - - - - -
go ____ my heart, My own Be - lov - - - - - - -

mi!
ed?

The Blind Girl's Song

from *La Gioconda*

AMILCARE PONCHIELLI

Vo - ce di don - na o d'an - ge - lo le
Ah! 'tis the voice of An - gel bright, Has

mi - e ca - te - ne ha sciol - to; Mi vie - tan le mie
caused my__ cru - el chains to sev - er, While my poor eyes, de -

allarg.

te - ne - bre di quel - la_ san - ta, di quel - la santa il vol - to.
void of_sight, Can see_ thy_ fea-tures, can see_thy fea-tures nev - er.

col canto   *morendo*

affrett.

Pu - re da me non par - ta - si, da me non
Yet I would of - fer, ere we part, A to - ken

a tempo
p   *affrett.*

rall.

par - ta - si, senza un pie - to - so don, no! no!_____ A
from my heart. from my sad, grate-ful heart! Ah! Ah!_____ This

col canto

a tempo

te que - sto ro - sa - ri - o che le pre - ghie - re a
ro - sa - ry I give thee, Round it my heart - felt

pp leggerissime

du - na,   Io te lo por-go, ac - cet - ta - lo, ti par - te -
prayers cling,   Deign to ac-cept the gift from me, It will good

rà   for - tu - na. _____   Sul - la tua te - sta
for - - tune to thee _____ bring: _____ And on thy head for

espandendosi

vi - gi - li la mia be - ne - di - zion, _____ sul - la tua
ev - er near, Shall be my heart - felt prayer! _____ shall be my

allarg. molto   a tempo

te - sta, sul - la tua te - sta vi - gi - li _____ la _____
prayer, _ shall be my heart - felt prayer, shall be _____ my _____

mi - a be - ne - di - zion,
heart-felt, my heart - felt prayer,

la mia be - ne - di - zion vi - gi - li,___ vi - gi -
shall be my heart-felt prayer, ev - er___ near,___ ev - er___

li, ah! sul - la tua te - sta vi - gi - li a mi - a
near, Ah! shall be my heart-felt prayer, shall be my prayer,

be - ne - di - zion._____
shall be my prayer!_____

163

Che Farò Senza Euridice

from *Orfeo*

C.W. VON GLUCK

Ahi - mè!   do - ve tra - scor - si,   o - ve mi
A - las!   why hast thou left me,   left me to

spin-se un de - li - rio d'a - mor?
suffer in a mad-ness of love?

Allegro.

Spo - sa...
Loved one!

Eu - ri - di - ce...   Eu - ri - di - ce...
Eu - ri - di - ce!   Eu - ri - di - ce!

Con - sor - te...   Ah! più non vi - ve... la
My own one!   She lives no longer,   I

chia-mo in-van!
call her in vain.

Mi-se-ro
O, what

me! la per-do e di nuo-vo e per sempre! oh leg-ge! oh mor-te! oh ri-
mis'ry to lose her a - gain and for ev-er! O judgment, O sad death, cru-el

cor - do cru - del! Non ho soc - cor - so... non m'a-van - za con-
re - col - lection! I have no help - er, naught gives me con - so -

siglio... io veggo so-lo (Oh__ fie-ra vi-sta!) il lut-tu-o-so aspet-to del-
lation, naught can I image, (O__ fearful vision!) naught but the dark, gloomy aspect, the

l'or-ri-do mio sta-to! Sa - zia-ti, sor-te re-a... son di-spera-to!
horrors of my being! Now fate may wreak her vengeance, I am despairing.

Allegretto.

Che fa - rò   senza Eu - ri - di - ce?   Do-ve an-drò   senza il mio
Live with - out   my Eu - ri - di - ce!   Can I   live   without my

ben?   Che fa - rò?___ Do - ve an - drò?___ Che fa - rò   sen - za il mio
love?   In my   woe,   where can I   go?___ Whith-er   wan-der___ with no___

ben?   Do - ve an - drò sen - za il mio___ ben?   Eu - ri -
love?   whith-er___ wan - der with no___ love?   Eu - ri -

di - ce! Eu - ri - di - ce! oh Di - o! ri - spon - di...
di - ce! Eu - ri - di - ce! Oh, Heav-en! now tell me,

Adagio.

ri - spon - - - di... Io_ son_ pu - re il tuo fe -
O tell_____ me, I_ am_ for ev-er thy true

p col canto

de - le, io son pu - re il tuo fe - del, il_ tu - o fe - de - le! Che fa -
lov-er, I_ am for_ ev - er thy true lov - er, true lov - er! Live with-

Tempo I.

rò senza Eu - ri - di - ce? Dove an - drò senza il mio ben? Che fa -
out my Eu - ri - di - ce! Could I live with-out my love? In_ my

f

167

rò?__ do - ve an - drò? che_ fa - rò sen - za il mio ben? Do - ve an-
woe, where can I go?__ Whither__ wan-der__ with no__ love, whither__

drò__ sen - za il mio__ ben? Eu-ri - di - ce! Eu-ri - di - ce!
wan-der__ with no__ love? Eu-ri - di - ce! Eu-ri - di - ce!

Moderato.

Adagio.

Ah! non m'a - van - za più__ soc - cor - so, piu spe - ran - za nè dal
Thro' darkness groping, no help giv - en, Noth-ing hoping from earth or

Tempo I.

mon - do, nè__ dal ciel! Che fa - rò senza Eu - ri -
heav - en, from earth or heav'n! Live with-out my Eu - ri -

di - ce? Dove an - drò senza il mio ben? Che fa - rò?_ Do - ve an -
di - ce! Whither wan - der with no love? In_ my woe, where can I

drò?_ Che fa - rò_ sen - za il mio ben? Do - ve an - drò?_ Che fa -
go?_ Whither_ wan - der_ with no_ love? Where can I go, in_ my

rò?_ Do - ve an - drò sen - za il mio ben, sen - za il mio ben,_____
woe?_ Whith - er_ wan - der with no_ love, with - out my_ love,_____

_ sen - za il mio ben?
_ with - out my love?

Tu Che Le Vanita

GIUSEPPE VERDI

Tu che le vanità conoscesti del mondo e godi nell' avel il riposo profondo, s'ancor si piange in cielo, piangi sul mio dolore, e porta il pianto mio al

You who knew world-ly pride, all the pomp life af-forded, En-joy your deep, long sleep by the grave thus re-ward-ed, If one may weep in Heav-en, Weep when you see my sorrow, Then take my tears before the

marcate   cresc.   grandioso

tro - no del Si-gnor,   il pian-to mi - o por-ta al
high throne of the Lord,   Take all my tears now to_ the

f   *sempre f*   *f*

tro - no_ del_ Si - gnor.
high throne of_ the Lord.

p

Allegro   **Recitativo**

Car - lo qui-ver - rà!
Car - lo will be here!

pp   *col canto*   *pp*

Si!   Che par-ta   e scor-da o-
Yes!   Then leav-ing,   he must for-

171

mai___ / get me!

A Po - sa di ve - gliar sui gior-ni suoi giu-rai.___ Ei
I vowed we'd nev-er part no mat-ter what be-set me. He'll

a tempo

Allegro moderato

se - gna il suo de - stin, la___ glo-ria il trac - ce - rà Per
fol - low his own fate, find___ glo - ry his ca - reer; For

me, la mia gior - na - ta a se - ra è giun - ta già!
me, the day is end - ed, and night's al - read - y here!

morendo

Vanne, Vanne

from *The Coronation of Poppea*

tù, che tan - to ce - le - bra - i.
time. *My act is brave and wor - thy.*

Bre - ve an - go - scia è la mor - te,
Death is not___ un - pleas - ant.

un so - spir pe - re - gri - no e - sce dal co - re
It re - leas - es the soul quick - ly from bond - age,

o - ve è sta - to mol - t'an - ni, qua - si in ho -
where for man - y long years it suf - fered and

spi - tio,
strug - gled,

co - me fo - ra - stie - ro,
cap - tured by the bod - y.

e se ne vo -
Now it may rise___

- la al - l'O - lim - po del - la fe - li - ci - tà sog - gior - no___ ve - ro.
toward O - lym - pus and find at last the sum - mit of hap - - pi - ness

174

Recit.   Moderato

I - te - ne tut - ti   a pre-pa-rar - mi il ba - gno,   che
E-nough la-ment - ing.   My fin-al bath is read - y.   For

se la vi-ta cor - re co-me ri - vo flu - en - te,   in un te-pi-do
life is like the wa - ter: it flows much too quick-ly,   and the hu - mors with-

ri - vo   que-sto san-gue in-no-cen-te io vo',___ vo' che va-da a im-por - po-
in me,   as they course through my bod - y and spread,_ form a tap-es-try made of

                                          rit.   Lento

rar - mi   del mo - rir,   del mo - rir   la stra - - da.
sil - ver,   which will help   me to die   with wis - - dom.

Habanera

from *Carmen*

GEORGES BIZET

Carmen

L'a-mour
Love is

est un oi-seau re - bel - le Que nul ne peut_ ap-pri-voi - ser, Et c'est
like an-y reb-el bird That none can ev - er_hope to tame; And in

bien en vainqu'on l'ap-pel-le, S'il lui con - vient de_ re-fu - ser. Rien n'y
vain is all woo-ing heard If he re-fuse_ your heart to claim. Naught a -

176

fait, me-nace ou pri è - re, L'un par - le bien__ l'au-tre se tait; Et c'est
vails, neith-er threat nor prayer, One speaks to me__ the__ oth - er sighs; It's the

l'au-tre que je pré - fè - re Il n'a rien dit;__ mais il me plait.__
oth - er that I pre - fer,__ Though mute, his heart__ to__ mine re - plies.__

L'a - mour!_____ l'a - mour!_____
Oh, love!_____ Oh, love!_____

l'a - mour!_____ l'a - mour! L'a-mour est
Oh, love!_____ Oh, love! A gyp-sy

en - fant de Bo - hême, Il n'a ja - mais, ja-mais con-nu de loi, Si tu ne
boy is Love, 'tis true, He ev - er was and ev - er will be free; Love you not

m'ai - mes pas, je t'ai - me; Si je t'ai-me, prends garde à toi!_____
me, then I love you,_____ If I love you, be-ware of me!_____

Si tu ne m'ai - mes pas, si tu ne m'ai-mes pas, je t'ai - me!
Love you not me,_____ love you not me, then I love you!_____

178

Mais si je t'ai - me, si je t'ai-me,prends gar - de à toi!
But if I love you, if I love you, Be - ware of me!

Si tu ne m'ai - mes pas, si tu ne m'ai-mes pas, je t'ai - me!
Love you not me, love you not me, then I love you!

Mais si je t'ai - me, si je t'ai - me,prends garde à toi!
But if I love you, if I love you, be - ware of me!

Reverie

Claude Debussy

182

Un Bel Di

from *Madame Butterfly*

GIACOMO PUCCINI

nu - to! Io non gli scen - do in - con - tro. Io no. Mi
told you! But I won't go to meet him. Not yet! I

Tempo I
con semplicità

met - to là sul ci - glio del col - le e a - spet - to, e a - spet - to gran
wan - der to the rim of the hill-top and wait there. I wait for a

tem - po e non mi pe - sa,_____ la lun - ga at - te - sa.
long time but I don't mind it,_____ I'm used to wait - ing.

animando un poco

E...u - sci - to dal - la fol - la cit - ta - di - na_____
A man e - mer - ges from the crowd - ed cit - y,_____

Tut - to que-sto av-ver - ra, te lo pro-met - to. Tien - ti la tua pa-
That's the way it will be, you may be-lieve me. You have no right to

u - ra, io con si - cu - ra fe - de l'a - spet - to.
doubt it while I with faith un-shak - en a - wait him!

poco rall. e cresc. Largamente

menof *dim.* *rit.*

pp sostenuto *mf* *p*

Abendlied

Felix Mendelssohn

1. Das Ta - ge-werk ist ab-ge -than. Gieb,
2. Wenn du ge-treu voll - en - det hast, wo -

Va - ter, dei - nen Se - - gen! Nun dür - fen wir der Ru - he nah'n; wir
zu dich Gott be - stell - te, be - hag-lich fühlst du dann die Rast vom

tha - ten nach Ver - mö - - gen. Die hol - de Nacht um -hüllt die Welt, und
Thun in Hitz' und Käl - - te. Am Him-mel glänzt der A - bend-stern und

Stil - le herrscht in Dorf und Feld.
zeigt noch bess'- re Rast von fern.

Amour, Viens Aider

from *Samson And Dalila*

CAMILLE SAINT-SAENS

Dalila

Sam- son ___ re-cherchant ma pré-
To - night!___ Samson makes his o-

sen _ ce, Ce soir doit ve-nir en ces lieux.
bei-sance, This eve at my feet he will lie;

Voi-ci l'heu-re de la ven-gean - ce Qui doit sa-tis-
Now the hour of my vengeance hast - ens: Our Gods I shall

192

Moderato (♩=92)

fai - re nos Dieux!
soon glo - ri - fy!

cresc.

f   *dim.*   *p*

Ped. ✳

A - mour! viens ai - der ma fai - bles - se!
O Love, of thy might let me bor - row!

Ver - se le poi - son dans son sein!   Fais que, vain-
Pour thy poi - son thro' Sam - son's heart!   Let him be

f   *p*

cu par mon a - dres - se, Sam - son soit en-chaî - né de-
bound be-fore the mor - row, A cap-tive to my match _ less

main!
art!

Il voudrait en vain _ de son â - me Pou-
In his soul he no long-er would cher - ish The

cresc. dim. p

voir me chasser, me ban-nir!
pas - sion he wish-es were dead;

cresc.

Pourrait - il é-tein-dre la
Can a flame like that ev - er

p

flam-me Qu'a-li - men-te le sou-ve - nir?
per - ish, Ev - er-more by remembrance fed?

dim. pp

Il est à
He rests my

194

moi! c'est mon es - cla - ve! Mes frè - res
slave; his feats be - lie him! My breth - ren

crai - gnent son courroux; Moi, seule en - tre
fear with vain a - larms, I on - ly, of

tous, je le bra - - - ve,
all, I de - fy -

ve, Et le re - tiens à mes ___ ge - noux!
him, I hold him fast with - in ___ my arms!

A - mour! viens ai - der ma fai -
O Love, of thy might let me

bles - se! Ver - se le poi - son dans son
bor - row! Pour thy poi-son thro' Sam-son's

sein! Fais que, vain - cu par mon a -
heart! Let him be bound be-fore the

dres - se, Sam - son soit en-chaî - né____ de -
mor - row, A cap - tive to my match - less

196

main!
art!

Con-tre l'a-mour sa force est
When love con-tends, strength ev-er

vai - ne;
fail - eth;

Et lui, le___ fort par-mi les
E'en he, though strong-est of the

forts,
strong,

Lui, qui d'un peu - ple rompt la
Thro' whom in war his tribe pre-

chaî-ne, Succom-be-ra___ sous mes ef-forts!
vail-eth, Will'gainst my charms not bat-tle long!

Romance

from *The Merry Widow*

FRANZ LEHAR

Love in my heart a-wak___ing, A rose_bud in__ the May, In_to full beau_ty break___ing, Be_came a rose to-day.___ I hard_ly mark'd it bud___ding To_wards the sun a-

198

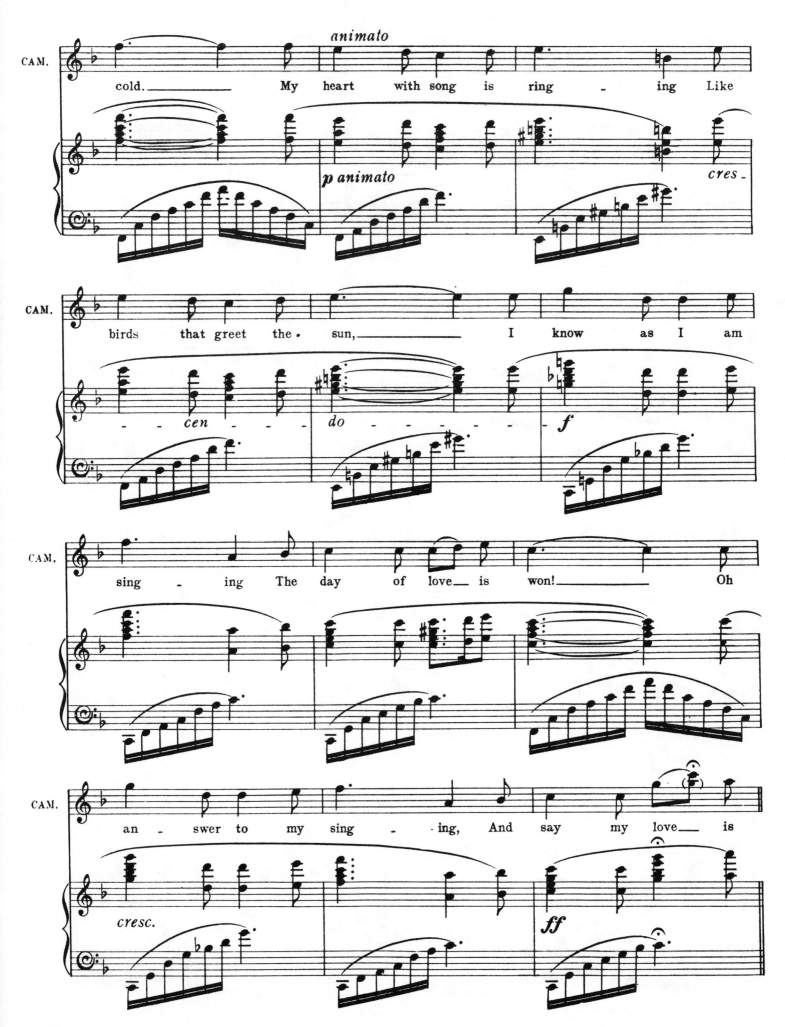

200

Allegretto

NATALIE

Oh, Ca＿mille!

CAM.

won! Nat＿a＿lie!

NAT.

animato

Ah! leave me, pray! I

animato *cres* ＿ ＿ ＿ *cen*

NAT.

know not what I shall do or say!

＿ *do* ＿ ＿

CAMILLE

Good＿bye, then, my dar＿ling— Give me one last

201

CAM. round, _____ There will love's light be found _____

lento
CAM. Come to the lit _ tle ar _ bour here __ There is no _ thing there to

Moderato
NATALIE.
CAM. fear, My dear! I

NAT. ought not Yet I can _ not re _ sist you!

NAT.

CAM.

Come to the lit_tle ar_bour here— There is no_thing there to

p a tempo

rit.

NAT. My dear!

CAM. fear, My dear!

Allegro

p

Ped.

ff

205

Toreador Song

GEORGES BIZET

207

208

O, Tsarevich, I Entreat You

from *Boris Godunov*

Larghetto amoroso (♩. = 50)

MODEST MUSSORGSKY

O, ца-ре-вичъ, у - мо-ля - ю, о, не кля-ни ме-ня за рѣ - чи
O, Tsar-e-vich, I en-treat you! For-give me, friend, be-cause my cru-el

злы-я, не у-ко-ромъ, не на-смѣш-кой, но чис-той лю-
words were not in-tend-ed, to be re-proach-es! It was my great

бовь - ю зву-чать о - нѣ, жаж - дой сла-вы тво-ей, жаж - дой ве-личь - я
love that drove me to speak thus; jeal - ous am I for your fame and your hon - or!

209

звучатъ о нѣ вѣ ти ши ноч-ной, мой ми лый. О, мой ко-
Now hear me, love, when night is dark and si - lent. O my be-

ха ный, не-из-мѣ нитъ тво-я Ма-ри-на! За-будь, о, за-
lov - ed, your Ma - ri - na will nev-er de-ceive you! For-get, for-

будь о ней, за-будь о люб-ви сво-ей; ско-рѣй, ско-рѣй на от-чій пре-
get her now! For-get her and love a-while, and go to seize your law - ful

столъ.
throne.

DMITRI

Ма-ри-на! Ад-ску-ю му-ку ду-ши мо-ей
Ma-ri-na! Hell has no tor-ture to e-qual mine!

210

M. Царь мой!
Tsar my own!

D. жизнь мо - я!
are my life!

MARINA

О, какъ серд - це мо - е о - жи -
Ah, you have brought me fresh hope and

DMITRI

Встань, ца - ри - ца мо - я не - на - гляд - на - я!
Rise, Tsar - i - tsa mine! Queen of my heart, a - rise!

M.

ВИЛЪ ТЫ, ПО - ВЕ - ЛИ - ТЕЛЬ

cour - age! Come, _____ my love, my

D.

Об - ни - ми ты же - лан - на - го, встань, об - ни -

Come to me, _____ my bride long de - sir'd, come _____ to

cresc.

M.

МОЙ!

King!

D.

МИ!

te!

f

Moderato maestoso (♩ = 100)

f

sf

sf

sf

213

Son Vergin Vezzosa

from *I Puritani*

VINCENZO BELLINI

Son ver _ gin vez _ zo _ sa in ve _ ste di spo _ sa, son

bian _ ca ed u _ mi _ le qual gi _ glio d'a_pril. Ho chio _ me o _ do_

_ro _ se cui cin _ ser tue ro_

se, tue ro _ _ _ se, ho il se _ no gen _ ti _ le del _ del tuo mo _

_ nil.

Son bianca e du _ mi _ le _ qual gi _ glio _ d'a _ pri _ le, _ son _

bian _ ca, sì, sì, sì. Son ver _ gin _ vez _ zo _ sa in

ve _ ste di spo _ sa, son bian _ ca ed u _ mi _ le qual gi _ glio d'a

_pril. Ho chio _ me o _ do _ ro _ se cui cin _ ser tue ro _

_ _ _ _ _ se, tue ro _ _ _ se, ho il se _ no gen _

_ti _ le del bel mo _

_nil, del_____ bel, del bel_____ mo _ nil.

Dim _ mi s'è ver che m'a _ mi? Dim _ mi s'è ver che m'a _ mi? Qual

mat _ tu _ ti _ na stel _ la bel _ la vogl'io bril _ lar: del crin le molli a _

_nel _ la mi gio _ va a daggra _ ziar, ad____ ag _

bel _ la, ti _ ce _ lo le a_nel _ la del _ crin, _____ co_ m'io ____ nel _ bel

ve _ lo mi vo _ glio ce _ lar. A _ sco _ sa, ___ vez_zo _ sa nel

ve _ lo, ___ nel ve _ _ _ _ _ _ _ lo di _

_vin _____ or sem _ bri_la spo _ sa che vas _ si all'al_tar.

219

Ah!__ se il pa_dre s'a_di_ ra, io vo_lo a mia stan_ _ _ _ _ _ _ _ _za.

Ah!__ ah! po_scia, o fe_del,__ tu

po _ sa _ mi il vel,

po _ sa il vel,   mi___ po _ sa il vel,   mi___

po _ sa il   vel.

Una Voce Poco Fa

from *The Barber Of Seville*

GIOACCHINO ROSSINI

vo _ ce po_co fa qui nel cor mi ri_suo_nò; il mio cor__ fe_ri_to è già, e Lin_

_dor__ fu che il pia_gò. Sì, Lin_do _ ro__mio__sa _ rà, lo giu_ra_i, la vin_ce_

_rò, sì, Lin_do _ ro__mio__sa _ rà, lo giu _ ra_i, la__vin_ce_

_rò. Il tutor ri_cu_se _ rà, io l'in_ge_gno aguz_ze_

_rò, al_la fin s'acchete _ rà e contenta io re_ste_rò... Sì, Lin_

223

-do - ro — mio — sa - rà,   lo giu - ra - i,   la — vin - ce - rò,   sì, Lin-

-do - ro — mio — sa - rà,   lo giu - ra - i,   la vin - ce - rò.